Broken
Poems from the Holy Spirit
By Julie Anshasi

Giant Publishing Company
Lincoln, Nebraska, USA

2017 by Julie Anshasi

Published by Giant Publishing Company
Post Office Box 6455
Lincoln, NE 68506
www.giantpublishingcompany.com

Printed in the United States of America

All rights reserved. No part of this publication may be used or reproduced in any form or by any electronic or mechanical means, including information storage and retrieval systems, without permission in writing from the publisher.

Library of Congress Cataloging-in-Publication Data
Anshasi, Julie, 1963 -
Broken – Poems from the Holy Spirit: poetry/Julie Anshasi
   1.   Poetry-Christianity
TXu 2-073-619
ISBN 978-0-9995873-0-0

Books by Julie Anshasi

Some Things are HOT! Some Things are NOT!
Copyright 2018

Behind the Word: Bible Stories to Ignite Your Imagination
Copyright 2018

Why Did the Dinosaurs Die?
Copyright 2019

Winter in Eden – Winner of the 2022 Illumination Book Awards Bronze Medal
Copyright 2020

The Revelation of Jesus Christ
Copyright 2020

One Part Nonsense
Copyright 2020

Spiritual Exhaustion
Copyright 2021 - Winner of the 2022 Illumination Book Awards Silver Medal

Forgiving Yourself
Copyright 2021

For the Holy Spirit.
Thank You for being my best friend.

Listing of poems

The Hand of God..Page 1
The house of God...Page 2
Victory...Page 3
Only God..Page 4
God's great mercy..Page 6
Second chance..Page 7
No tears in heaven...Page 8
Resurrection..Page 9
Face to face...Page 10
Whatever..Page 11
Mountain...Page 12
Love..Page 13
Rain...Page 14
Prodigal...Page 15
Longing...Page 16
No choice..Page 18
The garden...Page 19
The hound of heaven..Page 20
Faith..Page 21
Luke 17: 12-19..Page 22
Luke 18: 10-14..Page 24
Held by Him..Page 26
Your word...Page 27
God alone...Page 28
Trust – part 1..Page 30
Trust – part 2..Page 32
Courage..Page 33
Mark 5: 1-20...Page 34
Forgiveness..Page 36
Blue, gray, black...Page 37
The book...Page 38
John 8: 1-11...Page 40
I AM..Page 42

Listing of poems, continued

Come……………………………………………………Page 44
Believe…………………………………………………..Page 45
Walking on water………………………………………Page 46
Heaven's key……………………………………………Page 47
What will it be like? ……………………………………Page 48
Broken…………………………………………………..Page 50
Through the looking glass……………………………Page 52
When the tears stop falling…………………………Page 53
A changed mind……………………………………...Page 54
Rise……………………………………………………...Page 56
The only One…………………………………………..Page 59
God's path……………………………………………...Page 60
The woman at the well……………………………….Page 62
Reconciliation…………………………………………Page 64
Worth it…………………………………………………Page 66
The outcome is not up to you..……………………Page 67
Conscience…………………………………………….Page 68
Don't give up…………………………………………..Page 70
The end………………………………………………...Page 72
Don't let the devil win…………………………………Page 73
The battle……………………………………………..Page 74
The least of these……………………………………..Page 76
Walking, and leaping, and praising God…………..Page 78
James 4:7……………………………………………...Page 79
Deliverer………………………………………………..Page 80
Who You Are…………………………………………..Page 81
Mystery…………………………………………………Page 82
Abraham………………………………………………..Page 83
Always there…………………………………………...Page 84
Enough………………………………………………….Page 85
His Hands………………………………………………Page 86
Luke 7: 36-50………………………………………...Page 88
Liberty…………………………………………………..Page 90
His Heart………………………………………………..Page 92

Listing of poems, continued

Conformed to His image.................................Page 94
Pearl...Page 95
The stone..Page 96
My prayer...Page 97
Presence...Page 98
Psalm 2012...Page 100
My God..Page 101
Holy..Page 102
The Face of Jesus...Page 103
What the Lord has done..................................Page 104
The heavy cross..Page 105
Silence..Page 106
The lost sheep...Page 107
The good Samaritan.......................................Page 108
Suicide Bible..Page 110
Step of faith..Page 112
the lion/THE LION..Page 113
A stone..Page 114
Tender love...Page 116
Him...Page 117
Beautiful obedience..Page 118
The carpenter..Page 119
Risen...Page 120
The "bastard"..Page 122
The beauty of your absence............................Page 123
Bread...Page 124
Questions/Answers...Page 125
In heaven..Page 126
For Who You Are...Page 127
Dressed in glory...Page 128
Dead men's bones...Page 129
I know...Page 130
Don't worry..Page 131
For Isaiah..Page 132

Listing of poems, continued

For Zach...Page 134
For Jenna...Page 135
Mothers...Page 136
First in line..Page 138
My crown...Page 139
Stand..Page 140

The Hand of God

No more light, it's all grown dim,
His Voice is drowned out by the wind.
Flood waters rise, I cannot swim
To clutch the Hand of God.

The darkness closes all around,
And silence smothers every sound,
The weight has pushed me to the ground
Without the Hand of God.

I try to walk but don't know how,
Beneath the pressure I have bowed,
And Satan whispers: *Give up now!*
There is no Hand of God.

Yet dimly seen from far away:
A light reveals the dawning day.
I am so close, I hear Him say:
Just take the Hand of God.

With desperate cries and many tears
The darkness of a thousand years
Is swept away, with every fear -
All by the Hand of God.

At last, the peace I've waited for,
Just when I thought it was no more,
My boat has reached that tranquil shore.
I'm walking through His open door!
No longer weighted down, I soar!
HIS MERCY REIGNS FOREVERMORE!

THE MIGHTY HAND OF GOD.

The house of God

O mighty God, Who condescends,
To have this dust to be His friend.
All powerful, all knowing God.
Who walks with men on earthly sod.

Not satisfied to stay away,
He lives within this house of clay.
A makeshift shack for Deity,
A humble dwelling for a King.

A house of flesh for God?
How can it be?
The Maker of the heavens
Lives in me?

No mind can grasp, no man can know
His glory hidden in my soul.
He changes wretched men of sin
'Till face to Face, we look like Him.

O God, I am undone, undone!
Confronted with Your sinless Son.
He chose to make His home in me.
He chose me for His own, indeed.

A human house for God?
How can it be?
The Alpha and Omega
Purchased me.

Victory

The victory is Yours, O God.
Your Hands, I know, it holds.
The lies of Satan swept away
Your truth I see more, every day.

The victory is mine to grasp
No snare can hinder me.
The finish line is now in view
I'm pressing on to be with You.

You gave the victory to us,
With all the gifts You freely give,
And I can see Your Face unveiled
And know Your power will prevail.

O God, Your victory I need,
Your strength to finish all my tasks,
Your mighty Arm to hold me up,
Your healing oil to fill my cup.

Victory! Victory!
My hopeful heart does cry.
Forward! Forward! No turning back,
With Your supply, I cannot lack.

Only God

The miseries of human flesh,
The darkness, sickness, stench of sin,
The pain-filled days and weeping nights
Are swept away with sight of Him.

For only God can take a man
Depraved and filthy, rotten through.
Take from him his sinful self,
And make him into something new.

Only God can see the end
While stumbling, falling, on we crawl
Only God repairs the torn.
Only God can see it all.

All the sleepless nights!
All the wasted days!
Never looking up,
Blind to all His ways.

Missing every mark,
Losing ground each day.
Groping in the dark.
Wretched, blind, decayed.

Only God restores!
Only God can heal!
Only God can save!
Only God reveals!

Only God is sure!
Only God is just!
Only God is true!
Only God I trust!

Don't let the lies of Satan
Bind and shackle you.
Don't listen to his whispers.
Only God is true!

Don't take the tempter's offer
The wide and easy road
Turn back to your Great Father.
Release your heavy load.

Only God can do it.
Only God alone.
Only God is able
To break a heart of stone.

Only God's great mercy
Our every need supplies.
A miserable, crawling worm becomes
A gorgeous butterfly.

God's great mercy

God's great mercy falls like rain.
A healing balm to thirsty plains,
A shower of blessing to my soul -
My mercy cup now overflows.

God's great mercy, opened wide,
Rushes in a sweeping tide,
Overpowers my darkened soul,
Covers me and makes me whole.

What great mercy pardons me!
What matchless grace my eyes now see.
The punishment that should be mine,
Has been erased without a sign.

O God, Your ways I cannot know,
But on Your path my feet must go.
My God, my Savior, You alone!
Your grace, Your mercy lead me home.

Second chance

Cast out of Eden, banished from truth
Nowhere to turn for love.
Running away, hidden from view
But not from Him above.

O guilty one, you know inside
The sin that never leaves.
O sinful one, you try to hide
The shame that ever clings.

God in His mercy offers to you
A glorious second chance.
The second Adam gives to you
A pardon not of man.

Unworthy? Oh, yes, but still He gives
His love and pardon now.
Life from above you must now live,
His Spirit shows you how.

Eyes on Him, never looking away,
Blind to other offers.
Go to Him, and go today.
Back to your dear Father.

No tears in heaven

And God Himself shall wipe away
All tears from their eyes,
The torment, pain and misery,
The suffering and lies.

The former things are passed away,
Behold, all things are new.
For Christ has finished His good work
That He began in you.

O happy day! O glorious shore!
The shining city waits.
To be with Jesus evermore!
To meet Him at the gate.

Jesus, Messiah, Lord, and King,
Redeemer, and my Friend.
You've never turned Your Back on me,
Enduring till the end.

Jesus, Savior, my Rock, my all,
My comfort every day.
There are no tears in heaven, Lord.
You've wiped them all away.

Resurrection

Dead in the tomb, decaying,
A breathless, lifeless corpse,
Killed by the wages of sin,
And separated from Him.

But piercing through the darkness,
Corruption flees away,
His glorious light is shining,
Brighter than the morning.

Resurrection life imparted,
Raised from the dead, now alive.
The one who had no breath,
Is raised to life, from death.

Iniquity and its trappings,
Conquered and left in the tomb.
Sweetness and light replace,
Shadows that hid His Face.

O thank You, my precious Savior!
The resurrection and life.
Glory to Your holy Name!
I won't remain the same.

Face to face

If God be true, and every man a liar,
My thoughts must go to You God, ever higher.
The sin within me burnt out by Your fire,
Until the day I see You face to Face.

We are born in sin, and sinking day by day,
Without a Savior, humanity must pay
The debt of sin, too great for words to say.
But Jesus Christ has given us His grace.

Our sin becomes much more sinful, it is true
When through our darkness, we catch a glimpse of You.
When washed in Your blood, our souls are made brand new.
You take us to Your side, a glorious place.

O Jesus, what a great sacrifice for me!
My mind cannot comprehend the majesty.
That You would come and grant me Your victory,
Enabling me to finish every race.

Whatever

Whatever God asks of you,
He'll give you the strength to do it.
Wherever He tells you to go,
He'll show you the way to get to it.

Whatever God speaks to you,
He'll give you the ears to listen.
Whatever His place is for you,
He will make sure you don't miss it.

Wherever your eyes see a foe,
He'll turn them aside for you.
Whatever He wants you to know,
His Word has declared it is true.

Whatever He wants you to say,
His words will be very plain.
Your steps He has chosen each day,
In His presence you will remain.

So, go where He goes,
Say what He says,
Do what He wants you to do.
Stand on His Word,
Fight the good fight.
Remember His love for you.

Mountain

Towering far above my head,
This mountain is too big to climb.
I stand at the bottom and weep,
Knowing the sin that is mine.

I can't go over this mountain,
So big it is blocking my view.
I can't go through or around it.
There's only one thing I can do.

"Away with you, mountain!" I cry.
"Get out of my sight and my path!
There's no place for you in my life!
My present, my future, or past!"

When we use the faith He's given,
We call upon His holy Name,
Impossible things start to happen,
And sparks ignite into flames.

How easily mountains are moved,
How simply they bow to His will.
How perfectly problems are conquered.
How calmly our worries are stilled.

The Maker of heaven and earth,
The mountains and deserts and seas,
Has given His almighty power
To sinners like you and like me.

So, all my mountains are banished,
And troubles that rise up are quelled.
And sorrows and miseries vanish,
And giants with one stone are felled.

Love

God in His great mercy
Has given us His love.
No human mind can fathom,
It flows from Him above.

God in His great power
Has rescued you and me.
His strength throughout the ages
Unfolds for all to see.

Love one another daily,
And serve each other well.
Christ's sacrifice on the cross
Has saved us all from hell.

We love, for He first loved us,
With love we cannot grasp.
We must love each other now
With love that is steadfast.

The love I have for you, friend,
Day after day has grown.
Love enduring to the end,
And more than you can know.

Rain

Mercy falls like rain
On my thirsty soul.
Flooding me with grace,
And peace that overflows.

Rain on desert sands,
Rain on barren ground.
Rain on wilderness,
You're raining all around.

Sin had withered me.
Sin had parched me whole.
Sin had conquered me.
Till You reigned in my soul.

Drinking deep and full,
All from Your supply,
Drenched in mercy's rain,
No longer am I dry.

Jesus, O great Master!
Takes a wasted life,
Fills her with His rain,
And takes her as His wife.

A place where nothing grew,
Earth where nothing lived,
Bursts forth into life
With blessed rain He gives.

Prodigal

He stands and waits for His children,
Peering through mist, patiently.
He waits for the day we'll return
And a glimpse of our figure He'll see.

Often we carelessly wander,
So far from the Father we love.
Restlessly seeking another,
Believing that He's not enough.

His great wisdom allows us,
His children, to move from His side.
Never ceasing to love us.
Always wooing His bride.

Sin's consequences surround us,
When darkness has covered His Face.
His mighty Hand comes upon us.
And we see the meaning of grace.

We desperately run to our Father,
With tears and with sorrow so deep.
Knowing that we are unworthy,
Unable His precepts to keep.

But lovingly Father receives us,
And joyfully carries us home,
And ten thousand angels are singing,
No more from His presence we'll roam.

Longing

Give me ears to hear, Lord.
Give me eyes to see.
Don't let Your mysteries, Lord,
Remain unknown to me.

Penetrate this silence,
Feeble human realms,
Illuminate this darkness -
This empty place I dwell.

Hear, me, O my Maker,
Don't turn away from me.
Reveal to me Your presence,
That I may truly see.

God in all of heaven,
God in all of earth.
Your treasures are so boundless,
I cannot grasp their worth.

Change me, O my Master,
More and more each day.
Draw me to Your beauty,
Reshape this frame of clay.

God I cannot live here
Apart from Your great love.
Pull me ever nearer,
And up to things above.

Cleanse me from my sin, Lord.
Wash me in Your Blood,
Fill me with Your Spirit,
Release Your holy flood.

Jesus, precious Jesus,
I can't waste one day
Outside Your perfect presence,
Nor from Your path to stray.

Savior, loving Savior,
I give all to You.
I will not cease to follow
Until this life is through.

No choice

You know it's love
When He carries your cross for no reason
On a back stripped of flesh
from the scourge.

You see His love
When the blood runs down His beautiful Face
Where the thorns pierce His Skin
from a mocking crown.

You feel His love
When the soldier hammers home the nails
Through Hands that never did any wrong
and He hangs there for you.

Your soul bursts from love
When He shouts "It is finished!"
As darkness covers the earth, the veil rips in two
and the rocks break.

And you're undone by love,
Looking at Him,
With your heart laid bare -
Your sins destroyed.
You have no choice.

The garden

Quick to turn away,
To try to hide from You,
As if there was a place
Where we're not in Your view.

So ashamed of sin,
And running from Your gaze,
We turn our backs on You,
We try a different way.

You found us in the garden,
Exposed and shattered now.
You gently covered us,
By grace You showed us how.

Forced to leave Your garden,
Now wandering all alone,
We're overcome by fear,
We're very far from home.

Your Hand has never left us,
Our sinful, sorry state.
Your Eye is always on us,
And patiently You wait.

You keep drawing us,
Till we come back to You.
Your mercy covers us.
Your grace has made us new.

The hound of heaven

I pursue you.
I know your face and follow
Day and night.
You think you can hide
in many dark corners,
Yet I still shine My light.

I AM the hound of heaven,
I never give up your trail,
Day or night.
No matter how far away you go,
You're always in My sight.

I seek you out.
I want fellowship with you -
My delight.
I want you to know Me.
To win you I will fight.

My Eye is always on you,
Always looking in you -
Dark or light.
Never resting, never stopping,
Through depth and length and height.

Running after you -
Seeking you
With all My might.
Pulling you to Me -
Making your heart right.

Faith

Faith like a tumbling river,
Swept over me, up and away.
Tossed to and fro and gasping,
Surprised by the hope that He gave.

When we pray for an answer,
We often don't understand.
His answer is faith given to us,
He gives us the strength to stand.

The troubles we take to the Father,
Are swept away in faith's flood.
And nothing else seems to matter.
His grace is always enough.

My mountainous problems diminish,
My sorrows now seem very small.
When shown in the light of His glory,
My troubles don't matter at all.

I don't fear the fiery arrows
Their power to hurt me has dimmed.
And even though He may slay me,
Yet will I trust in Him.

Luke 17: 12 - 19

I was the leprous one.
I could not come close to You.
The filth that covered my soul
Held me apart from You.

I saw You passing by,
And I stood so far away.
"Jesus, O Master!" I cried.
"Have mercy on me today!"

One word from the Master,
And just one glimpse of His Face,
Simply His passing shadow,
And every stain is erased.

"Go show yourself," He said.
And that is just what I did.
But as I walked away,
I turned and went back to Him.

"Jesus, Lord," I whispered.
"Thank You for what You have done.
You've cleansed me from head to toe.
And I've received Your pardon."

Now all the world will know
What Jesus has done for me.
I will never be silent!
My Jesus has rescued me.

What is too hard for God?
What is it that He can't do?
Chains that we could never break
Fall off as He comes in view.

Any problem too much?
Or any mountain too high?
Satan's devices too strong?
That He can't sweep them aside?

All things are possible,
There's nothing that He can't do.
All that His word has promised,
Jesus will do it for you.

Give your problems to Him,
Simply trust and obey.
Power is yours if you ask.
Won't you ask Him today?

Luke 18: 10 - 14

Standing in Your temple,
I could not look at You.
Shattered by my failures,
Afraid what You might do.

I could barely whisper,
"Be merciful to me!
I am such a sinner!"
I know I'm not worthy.

The righteous man beside me,
Despised me for my sin.
I heard him praying loudly,
But I could not begin.

I could not lift my eyes,
Nor lift my weary head.
I simply cried to You,
And this is what You said:

"You are justified, child -
Your humbleness has shown:
You know you need a Savior,
You know you can't atone.

"I have justified you,
And I have made you whole.
All your sins are pardoned,
You now in peace may go."

We cannot understand Him -
The fullness of His grace,
The vastness of His mercy,
The beauty of His Face.

We cannot comprehend Him,
His never-ending love.
The glory of His pardon,
His majesty above.

A sinner comes to Him -
In desperation cries,
And Jesus pulls him closer,
And all his tears, He dries.

Now free to live in peace,
Now free to lift my head,
Glorious deliverance
Gives life to what was dead.

Held by Him

The wandering fatherless,
The blind and deceived helpless,
The ones who cry out for mercy -
The children who have no rest.

Jesus will not forsake them,
Jesus will not lose sight of them.
Jesus holds each one near -
His Hand is what's holding them.

His Hands bear each one's likeness,
So tightly does He grasp us,
So lovingly held by Him -
Receiving the Father's best.

For us He hung on the cross,
He chose to save all the lost,
He left His glorious home.
And paid the ultimate cost.

Now we are the children of God,
For us, against Satan, He fought.
Wandering and blind no more -
Redeemed by the One Who sought.

Your word

Your word, O Lord, is sweet.
Sweeter than honey to me.
Your words are a light to my soul,
And ever a lamp to my feet.

Guiding me on life's path,
Your word protects me from harm.
Sharper than any sword,
Cutting through Satan's swarm.

Your word hides in my heart,
That I might not sin against You.
With this, Your sword, in my hand,
I'll thrust the enemy through.

Your word's precious to me,
I long for it night and day.
I long for Your word to indwell me,
To hear all You have to say.

Write Your words in my heart,
Engrave Your words in my mind.
Equip this soldier to fight,
From each side, front, and behind.

Your word is ever true,
Your word is a constant friend,
Your word is ancient and new,
Your word endures to the end.

God alone

Who called creation into life?
Who gave the blinded eyes their sight?
Who turns the enemy to flight?
Only God alone.

Who gave the lifeless clay His breath?
Whose power has no height or depth?
Who pulled the sinner out of death?
Only God alone.

Who changed the sinful heart of man?
Whose sovereign gaze his mind has spanned?
Who plucked him from the liar's hand?
Only God alone.

Whose Fist has crushed the evil one?
Who placed His Spirit on His Son?
Who made the darkness as the sun?
Only God alone.

Who stripped away the veil from me?
Who made my eyes at last to see?
Who pardoned me at Calvary?
Only God alone.

Who creates love where there was none?
Who makes the lame get up and run?
Who fights all battles? Who has won?
Only God alone.

Who filled my empty soul with peace?
Who from my debts, had me released?
Who made the demons' torment cease?
Only God alone.

Who welcomes me with open arms?
Who shields me from all my alarms?
Who rescues me from every harm?
Only God alone.

Who gives me strength to run the race?
Who all my doubts with faith replaced?
Who holds me in His sweet embrace?
Only God alone.

Trust – part 1

Can I trust You, Lord?
Above all things on earth?
Above all human knowledge?
Beyond all that has worth?

Do I trust You, Lord?
When everything is gray?
When silence all around me
Obscures the words You say?

Will I trust You, Lord?
When You have broken me?
When all my shattered pieces
Are lying at Your Feet?

Can I trust You, Lord?
When I don't understand?
When all the things I've treasured
Have fallen from my hands?

Do I trust You, Lord?
Can You remove my fears?
Can You dispel the darkness?
Can You dry all my tears?

Yes, I trust You, Lord.
You, above all others.
You alone are faithful.
Closer than a brother.

Yes, I trust You, Lord -
Trust for anything.
Trust with all my might,
Trust in everything.

Yes, I trust You, Lord.
Every word You say.
Trust all that You're doing,
Trust You every day.

Trust – part 2

Trust is what kills the dragon,
Trust forces him to his knees.
Trust sends the enemy fleeing,
Causes Satan's torment to cease.

When we trust Almighty God,
No power in hell can stand.
No wicked device can flourish,
And Satan does not have a chance.

Our trust sends a message to Satan:
"We know One much stronger than you.
Your devilish plans will crumble.
There's nothing that He cannot do."

We trust Him for salvation,
Our souls are not left in the grave.
He delivers us from all evil.
His Hand is mighty to save.

Trust Him for deliverance,
For power, in word and in deed.
For love and for faith and for comfort,
For everything that we need.

Courage

Courage to face the devil and win -
Courage to break the bondage of sin,
Courage to reach up and grab hold of Him -
He gave that courage today.

I have courage to get up and fight,
I have courage to stand in the Light.
Courage to walk by faith, not by sight.
He gave that courage to me.

I will defeat the enemy's plans,
I will run over the enemy's lands,
I will claim victory over that man,
With courage God granted me.

Courage gives me the strength to go on,
Courage from Jesus rights every wrong,
Courage will shout: "Go forward! You've won!"
Courage that He gave to me.

I will not quit nor shirk the attack.
Courage has broken the enemy's back.
Courage makes demons fall in their tracks.
God's courage is mine today.

Satan, defeated, will fall on his face,
I will go on to finish the race,
Courage will go with me every place
That God has sent me to be.

Mark 5: 1 - 20

Naked and wounded, and mad,
Living among the tombs.
Cutting myself and screaming,
Darkness, despair and doom.

Tormented and taunted by demons,
Stumbling over the graves.
No man could hold me at all,
Nobody's hand could save.

But Jesus came near me one day,
He stretched out His Hand to me.
And all in one moment they left me,
And I was finally free.

Seated and clothed at His Feet,
And finally in my right mind,
Calmly I listened to Him.
For the first time I left fear behind.

Everyone saw me and marveled,
For what a change God did in me!
No longer insane and tormented,
I sit at the Savior's Feet.

Can God take a miserable sinner,
And wash him in heaven's rain?
And purge him from every demon,
Restoring his mind again?

Can God sweep away all the darkness?
That covers a body and soul?
And shine with His glorious light,
And make every broken man whole?

Oh, yes, God can do this and more.
Beyond all we ask or think.
God will heal all diseases,
And pull a man back from the brink.

God will renew everything,
If only we ask Him to,
God will restore every heart.
God will make everything new.

Forgiveness

Open the door and walk through it.
The door marked "Forgiveness" above.
Take one small step into grace,
And learn that His grace is enough.

Open the door and walk through it.
The door with His power to heal.
Take that step of forgiveness.
And walk into what He's revealed.

Forgiveness has lit up the way
Of even the most darkened path.
Forgiveness has helped us to say:
"I will not hold onto the past."

Jesus said: "Father forgive them.
For they do not know what they do."
His love covers every man's sins -
Rebuilds broken things inside you.

Forgiveness shouts: "It is finished!"
The dead ones rise out of their graves.
Forgiveness has opened the door,
His mercy walks through it to save.

Open the door of forgiveness.
Just open it, fling it out wide.
Let Jesus walk through to meet you,
And go to the other side.

Blue, gray, black

Midnight sky -
Blue, gray black,
Obscures the One Who made it.
You are there in the silence,
When all my prayers have faded.

When I seek You, You are there.
When I turn away, You are there.
Never changing, always present,
You are there.

I cry out to You.
My tears flood my pillow.
You always hear me.
You are always there.

When You answer me, You are there.
When You don't, You are there.
Visible? I take Your Hand.
Hidden? I can't understand.

But, You are always there,
Covered in the blue, gray, black.
Even if I turn my back –
You are there.

The book

Can blinded eyes be re-opened
With a mixture of spit and clay?
Can five little loaves and fishes
Feed five thousand men in a day?

Can man be formed out of dust,
Becoming a living soul?
The universe fashioned from nothing,
A paralyzed man be made whole?

Can thousands of people cross over
The sea and walk on dry land?
Can water come out of a rock
And spill on the desert sand?

Can a man fly to God in a whirlwind,
Never having to die?
Can one simple man build a boat
That rescues God's eight chosen lives?

Can eighty-five thousand soldiers
Be defeated by three hundred guys?
Can water and ox be consumed
By fire that comes from the sky?

Can demons be thrust from a man,
Leaving him sane and whole?
Can one giant fall from a stone
One shepherd boy did throw?

Can one perfect Man die for all,
And take on Him every man's sin?
Can one sacrifice be enough
To conquer Satan, and win?

Can Jesus, ALMIGHTY GOD!
Care about you and me?
Cry every tear that we cry,
And rejoice when we believe?

Can those who are dead rise again?
With life never taken away?
Can God in His mercy and power,
Restore all the devil has slain?

There aren't enough books to contain
The miracles He has done.
There's not enough time in the day
To speak of the power of the Son.

The rest of my life I'll spend telling
Everything God's done for me.
My story will join all the others
In God's book of eternity.

John 8: 1 - 11

Caught in the very act –
Stripped of all decency.
Everyone gathered like vultures
To watch the slaughter of me.

Without a doubt, guilty.
I can't move beyond this.
No way to undo what I've done
And find the mark that I've missed.

Watching the crowds gather,
I see stones in their hands.
Knowing that everything's finished.
Dying inside from my sin.

I heard it, far away,
Words like nothing I'd known.
"He who's without sin among you -
Let him cast the very first stone."

No one there could reply,
Conviction caused regret.
And one by one they all left me,
Till He was the only One left.

"Does no one condemn you?"
The Voice tenderly said.
"No one, My Lord," I said, weeping.
In shame I could not lift my head.

"Neither do I condemn,"
The Savior said to me.
"Go home now, and sin no longer."
And just like that - I was made free.

What power can pardon
These vile and filthy crimes?
What does it take to realize
The cleansing I now have inside?

Jesus of Nazareth knew,
He passed it on to me.
The human heart is so wicked -
More wicked than any can see.

All have sinned and fall short
Of God's glorious plan.
No human life can attain this -
The beautiful life of One Man.

Jesus poured out His blood
Freely for you and me.
So we can stand before Father,
Now knowing that we are redeemed.

Now I will sin no more,
I've seen the Savior's Face.
For everything in me has changed –
I now know the meaning of grace.

I AM

I spoke the word and it came into being.
I hung the moon and stars in space.
From emptiness formed the planets and sun,
And set the world in its place.

I made the oceans, mountains and plains.
I made the sky and the earth.
From nothing I fashioned the flowers and trees,
Lovely as music and verse.

I breathed into dust and created a man.
I put him over it all.
From heaven on earth, as he disobeyed,
I watched the universe fall.

I wept with Adam for such a great loss.
I covered him, hiding his sin.
From paradise lost, to shame and sin found,
From the garden I banished him.

I AM all knowing, I AM all seeing.
I know the end from the start.
I know there's nothing inside of man
To remedy his faithless heart.

I made mankind in the image of GOD
And now is the time to give -
The perfect Man to replace what was lost,
To rescue him where he lives.

I sent My blameless Son, Jesus, to you,
To repair the damage of man,
To renew every heart blackened by sin,
To restore everyone to Him.

I AM the Alpha, Omega and Lord.
I AM the still, small voice.
I AM the Maker of all that you see.
I place before you a choice.

Live in this forsaken world all alone -
Or turn to Jesus, My Son.
From sin and despair, to glorious hope,
Receive the work that He's done.

I AM JEHOVAH, author of life.
I AM THAT I AM, I say.
I AM everything you'll ever need.
The Truth and the Life, and the Way.

Come

For all who live in the dark,
For all who simply can't see.
For all whose hearts have been crushed
By Satan, our enemy.

Jesus says: "Come to the Light.
Come to My glorious throne.
Lay down your burden and come.
This is the place you belong."

Human minds just can't grasp it,
But simply come anyway.
Don't wait till you understand!
And don't wait another day!

The God of the universe
Who made it all with one breath,
Can bring everyone to Him,
And pull a man out of death.

Just listen, obey and trust.
Take a step forward in faith.
If you don't understand it,
His truth still remains unchanged.

God, Who makes things from nothing -
Can make something out of you.
Replacing your empty heart
With love and with faith anew.

Believe

Believe in the power of Almighty God,
All of the universe formed by His thoughts.
Faith He will give to all who are lost.
If only they will believe!

Believe in His majesty, mercy and grace.
Power to change you, your sins to erase,
Glorious light that shines from His Face,
You only have to believe!

With faith like a mustard seed, simply believe.
Your scars He will heal, your burdens relieve.
All of His mercy - yours to receive,
If only you will believe!

Believing in all that He has done for you -
Everything faded, His grace will renew.
There is no end to what He can do!
If only people believe.

Believe in the cross and its power today.
Believe in the One - He's mighty to save.
Believe with your heart -your mind will obey.
God simply tells you: Believe.

Walking on water

I can walk on the water,
If I only step out to meet Him.
And mountains move out of my way
With faith that He has given.

Walking on water with Him,
The easiest thing I've ever done.
I keep my eyes on the Savior
And over the waves I run.

Even the wind obeys Him,
Even rain and roaring waves are stilled.
All of the forces of nature
Must bow to His holy will.

Miracles, signs and wonders
Will follow everyone who believes.
Jesus, the One Who made it all -
All of His faith I receive.

Walking on water, oh, yes.
I must never stop looking at Him.
Move forward one step at a time,
Never to sink or to swim!

Jesus, Who walked on water,
Jesus, Who calmed the storm,
Jesus, Who granted me faith,
Jesus, Who's leading me home.

Heaven's key

Moved by a love so captivating -
Love for a world that was lost,
Jesus took every sin in His hands -
Hands that were nailed to a cross.

Filled with a love beyond human thought -
Love for the sinners like me,
Jesus paid every debt with His blood -
And left it at Calvary.

He shed His blood upon that bleak hill -
The place of the skull, they say.
He gave up the ghost in one last breath,
Satan defeated that day.

Broken and battered, bleeding for us -
He didn't refuse the cup.
Now joyfully we can come to Him,
His sacrifice is enough.

Almighty God, clothed in human flesh -
So loved the world in its shame,
Determined to bridge the gap between
Holiness and sinful man.

Now I can shout: Death, where is your sting?
Grave, where is your victory?
One spotless Person has died for us all,
In His Hand is heaven's key.

What will it be like?

What will it be like?
When You have come inside.
When all the world will know,
In me is where You hide.

What will it be like?
Your fullness to receive.
My sinful nature gone,
And glory shines through me.

What will people say?
When I'm no longer here.
When dark is stripped away,
And brilliant light appears.

What will be inside?
When all the sin is gone.
When every bit of You
Replaces all my wrong.

How will I appear?
To those who look at me.
No longer wrapped in flesh,
But clothed in majesty.

What will it be like?
When You have come again.
And changed me in a twinkling,
No longer fallen man.

What will it be like?
To have the Living God,
Make His home in me,
And make my thoughts His thoughts.

What will I do then?
When I'm at last like You.
Seeing face to Face,
And knowing all Your truth.

What will it be like?
To stand before Your throne.
And casting down my crown,
To know that I am home.

What will it be like -
To spend eternity,
With holy sovereign GOD
Here inside of me?

Broken

They didn't break Your Bones.
They didn't have to.
Your Heart wrenched within You
As the cock crew.

Betrayed and deserted
By Your dearest friends.
They could not watch one hour
Until the end.

Where were those who followed
God's great Messiah?
In deserted darkness
Left You to die.

You knew what You came for,
How the end would be.
Alone, misunderstood,
Accused falsely.

You answered not a word.
You didn't have to.
God needs no counselor.
Nothing to prove.

Wounded for transgressions,
And bruised for our sins.
Executed by lies
And hanged by them.

Maybe when the rocks split,
When the sky grew dark,
Maybe when the veil ripped
You changed their hearts.

It always takes the death
Of beautiful things
To make us finally see
What's been unseen.

God Himself became man
Did away with sin.
And rose to life, from death
So we could live.

Dead seeds planted in earth
Become something else.
And poverty's exchanged
For sudden wealth.

Through the looking glass

Hands upon the mirror,
Face against the glass,
Looking for my Savior,
His Face to see at last.

Lord, I want to see You -
Not what others see.
Not this fleshly image
Reflected back at me.

Seen through a glass darkly
Glimpses of Your Face.
Tiny bits of Jesus.
Bright shimmers of Your grace.

Lord, I want to see You
Over all of me.
Wood overlaid with gold,
Divine humanity.

Seen through the looking glass
Everything is dim.
But seeing face to Face,
Everything is Him.

Jesus, change my image
Into Yours divine.
Transform this human soul,
'Till it's no longer mine.

I want to look like Jesus,
Him I want to see.
Holy, precious Savior
Now looking back at me.

When the tears stop falling

When the tears stop falling -
When You've wiped them all away,
With the saints that live in glory,
I will stand and hear You say:
"Well done, faithful servant.
By My grace you've entered in.
No more buried talents,
And no more foolish sin."

When the tears stop falling,
And we stand before Your throne,
And we hear the angels singing,
Highest praise to You alone.
Everyone is shouting
"Hallelujah to the Lamb!"
Jesus, King of kings,
Son of God and son of man.

When the tears stop falling,
We will stand along the shore,
With the bells of heaven ringing,
And we all walk through The Door.
And every knee is bowed,
And every hand is raised,
And every tongue will shout
Glory to Your holy Name!

A changed mind

Repentance means I do not stay
In sin and darkness every day.
I turn and go the other way,
For You have changed my mind.

Repentance means I cannot bear
To live in shame and dark despair
Beneath a load of heavy cares
For You have changed my mind.

Repentance means I don't go back
And wander on the faithless track
Remembering everything I lack
For You have changed my mind.

Repentance means I turn around,
Come over to Your holy ground.
I once was lost, but now am found,
For You have changed my mind.

Repentance means I stand with You
Against the devil and his crew.
A blackened heart has been made new,
For You have changed my mind.

Repentance means I have the name
Of Jesus, and I'm not the same.
On my account, there is no blame,
For You have changed my mind.

Repentance means a brand-new life -
You've taken me to be Your wife.
The sinful man, no more alive!
PRAISE GOD! You've changed my mind.

Rise

Bloody sweat rolled down,
While earnest prayers went up.
An angel came to Him
And helped Him hold the cup.

Lord, I'll do Your will.
It's what I've always done.
Lord, I know the way
You've chosen for Your Son.

Lanterns, torches, weapons,
A friend's sword drawn in haste.
Growing in the darkness -
A multitude of hate.

Lord, I'll let them lead Me
Into Pilate's court.
Lord, I'll let them beat Me
While crowds around Me roar.

No charge laid against Him,
Nothing that would stand.
So Satan's lies were placed
On an innocent Man.

Lord, I'll let them mock Me,
Spit and slander too.
Lord, I'll let them tie Me
To the cross, for You.

Now His friends, returning,
Are weeping all around.
"Spare Him!" they were crying.
"Crucify him!" drowned them out.

Lord, I feel You with Me,
As the nails are hammered in.
"ELI!"
But....You've left Me -
As I became their sin.

Heaven weeping for Him,
Gathered at His cross.
Every heart is breaking.
Everything seems lost.

Lord, I know it's finished -
The work I came to do.
Father, God, I've given
My Spirit back to You.

Darkness smothered crosses,
Earthquakes shook the land.
No one understanding
Jehovah's sovereign plan.

Lord, I'll roll away
The stone in front of Me.
Lord, they'll see My scars,
And finally they'll believe.

To witness execution
Of Savior, Lord, and Friend -
To see Him now returning,
And know it's not the end!

Lord, I've spoken to them
The words I spoke before.
Lord, You'll send Your Spirit,
And they will know for sure.

Jesus, I'll not doubt You.
I've seen with my own eyes.
Death has been defeated,
And I, like You, will rise.

The only One

Your heart has broken, shattered, failed within you.
Your miseries have swept your life away.
Your human strength is gone, you cannot stand.
Why do you doubt the only One Who can?

Your tears have fallen till you're drowned in them.
Your sins have mounted up and covered you.
You cannot stand upright, a sinful man.
Why do you doubt the only One Who can?

Every sin, every fault and past mistake -
The accuser's thrown them all back at you.
These trespasses no human hands can mend.
Why do you doubt the only One Who can?

Attacked by enemies on every side,
Knowing in your heart that you must pardon.
The power to forgive? Not in your hands.
Why do you doubt the only One Who can?

The broken path you follow seems so hard.
You're frightened by the things that you have seen.
You don't know how to make a perfect plan.
Why do you doubt the only One Who can?

He's changing you each day to be like Him,
And bit by bit transforming things in you.
No work you do can raise your fallen man -
Don't ever doubt the only One Who can.

God's path

From my own road, and my own ways,
The Savior, with His staff,
Turned me around and pointed me
A new way, to His path.

Reversal of my former self -
A turnaround of ways.
From human fate and man's design -
From sin, to glory days.

When Satan lays a snare for you
To catch you in his grasp,
Reverse your steps and turn to God,
Expose that wicked trap.

His evil plans God has laid waste,
And every trap he lays,
Will spring before your feet are caught -
You've gone a different Way.

Fortune, fate, or random chance?
Or human cleverness?
Or is it God's path marked for you
That leads to peace and rest?

Satan's path is wide and smooth,
An easy one to follow.
And you and I can't see ahead
Nor see its snares tomorrow.

Turn around and choose The Way
(It might have bumps and stones.)
His rod and staff will comfort you
And guide you on toward home.

The woman at the well

Scorching heat
Heavy pot
Dusty road.
Whispered glances
Fleeting shadows
All alone.

Trudging forward
Getting water
Is my task.
Then I see Him
Living water
Hear Him ask.

Scorching shame
Heavy burdens
Many cares.
Tender questions
Loving answers
Healing there.

Running homeward
Telling all
What He's done.
Seeking water,
Finding Jesus –
He's the One.

Burdens lifted
Darkness fleeing
Glory shines.
Shame now vanished
Peace descending
Hope is mine.

His disciples
Bringing bread
Mystified.
Bread from heaven
(Sinners turning)
Satisfied.

Reconciliation

Dead in sin and trespasses,
Strayed from heaven's plan.
Sin has separated us -
God, from sinful man.

We are all disqualified
For evil dwells in us.
A chasm opened up between
Holiness and dust.

What does it take to bridge the gap
Between God and our sins?
The Holy One who lives above
Mankind's foolish whims?

Reconciliation brings
A sinner to his knees.
Knowledge of His saving grace
Makes blinded eyes to see.

A righteous man falls seven times
And gets back up again.
Forgiven when our sins return
Seventy times seven.

His love is unconditional
Wherever sin is found,
That is where His mercy's shown -
Grace much more abounds.

You can't earn His righteousness.
It is His gift to you.
Just one way you can receive -
One thing you can do.

Turn around and look at Him.
Your pardon He has planned.
Lift your head, reach up to Him
And take the Savior's Hand.

Worth it

It will all be worth it,
To be with You someday,
To walk that Street of gold,
Because You are the Way.

It will all be worth it,
To hold the Savior's Hand,
To see His precious Face,
And see that holy land.

It will all be worth it,
To bow before the King,
To join the angels singing,
And lay down everything.

It will all be worth it,
When all the tears are dried.
I'm face to Face with Jesus,
I'm standing at His side.

It will all be worth it,
No more fear and pain.
No more death and sickness,
No more sin and shame.

It will all be worth it,
And I can hardly wait.
To see my home in heaven,
To meet Him at the gate.

The outcome is not up to you

Walking by faith, and not by sight -
For flesh, it's not easy to do.
If you do what you know is right,
The outcome is not up to you.

Abraham went out, led by God,
Not sure what God wanted to do.
God said, "You shall be a blessing."
The outcome is not up to you.

How can you trust when you can't see
The things God is taking you through?
Your human mind may never know -
The outcome is not up to you.

You might be thrown into the fire,
Those who understand may be few.
It might make no sense at all, but -
The outcome is not up to you.

Trust in Jesus and move ahead.
Remember He makes all things new.
Knowing that He controls it all,
Thank God! It is not up to you.

Conscience

I spent my life stoning Your people,
Righteously consenting to their deaths.
Always sure I was doing Your will.
Quite proudly, Your laws I kept.

But You saw it differently, O Lord,
So You blinded me with Your great Light.
You knocked me down on Damascus road,
And from me, You took my sight.

I never meant to persecute You.
I always thought I knew what was best.
I pushed away my conscience from me -
But couldn't find any rest.

What do You want me to do now, Lord -
Now that my self-righteousness has slain
Innocent people who loved You, Lord -
Can I turn around again?

It's so hard for me to kick against
My conscience constantly pricking me.
But how am I supposed to change now
The things I've always believed?

What's that, Lord? I'm a chosen vessel?
You have marked me out to do Your will?
You know I'm a self-righteous killer.
And yet, You've chosen me still?

God took a proud and arrogant man -
Blinded him, then gave him back his sight.
Erased the self-righteous murders from
This man with the brand-new eyes.

Do we think we're doing Father's will
By stoning those who see other things?
Refusing to forgive when we're wronged -
Ignoring our conscience stings?

The Holy Spirit speaks to us through
Our conscience, shining His holy Light
On all the things He wants us to do -
Showing us each wrong and right.

What He has asked us to do, we must,
And not hesitate for a moment.
He'll give new eyes, and a brand-new name -
The clean conscience He has shown.

Don't give up

He's called you to a certain task,
And you must do what He has asked,
So just go on and don't look back.
Don't give up.

You don't know why He's chosen you,
Nor all the things that you should do,
Though overwhelmed, you follow through.
Don't give up.

You follow where He leads, but then,
The disapproving words of men,
Cause you to question what He said -
Don't give up.

So very hard to do the things
The Holy Spirit's prompting brings
The flesh rebels, and you can't see!
Don't give up.

Day after day, you stumble on.
You don't know if you're right or wrong,
And every hour seems much too long.
Don't give up.

When you're so spent you cannot stand,
Keep holding to the Savior's Hand.
The strength you need, your God will grant.
Don't give up.

Endure until the end, said He.
Just run the race and you will see,
You've got a crown of victory.
Don't give up.

The end

He stands at the end.
The end of all my plans,
The end of human strength,
And carnal thoughts of man.

He's my destiny.
I turn my feet toward Him.
Even if He's hidden,
From human eyes of sin.

He shows me one step.
He doesn't show me more.
After that one's taken
(And not one step before),

He will lead me on
One small step at a time.
He makes me walk by faith,
And not by human sight.

I must never fret,
Or worry where He leads.
First, I must obey Him.
And then His plan I'll see.

He stands at the end,
And I must go to Him.
I will see His purpose,
With eyes no more of sin.

Don't let the devil win

Pressed beyond measure, I can't go on.
I don't know how to begin.
God said, "Child, the end's in sight.
Don't let the devil win."

Satan comes to steal, kill and destroy.
Now I face his evil grin.
Stumbling on, I swing my sword.
Don't let the devil win.

So many times his darts pierce me through.
He reminds me of my sin.
Though he still accuses me,
Won't let the devil win.

My Jesus I must see face to Face.
Tempted like me, He has been.
If I run or only crawl,
Don't let the devil win.

We must not ever quit the battle -
Give up praying, seeking Him.
Lay down weapons in defeat?
Don't let the devil win!

Jesus, I will never stop fighting
For Your cause - now and again.
I will give my life for You.
Won't let the devil win.

The battle

Attacked on every side,
Flaming arrows, fiery darts.
The enemy takes aim,
Piercing through my heart.

Alone, I'm left alive,
And now they're seeking my life.
Left bleeding by the road,
Hacked by Satan's knife.

Jesus, I'm Your soldier.
Fighting battles, this I choose.
Satan has me cornered,
Broken, bloody, bruised.

Temptation's very strong
To lay all my weapons down.
Give up and surrender -
Forfeiting my crown.

I will not stop fighting,
Although mortal flesh is tired.
Step by step move forward,
Walking through the fire.

Endure until the end -
It's what I have been called to.
Use the sword You gave me,
Shield and helmet, too.

Push back Satan's forces
Till my General shouts, "All's well!"
Satan and his minions
Chased back into hell.

The least of these

I saw the Lord on His throne,
And all the angels with Him.
Each nation stood before Him
As He talked about their sin.

All His sheep are on one side
The goats are on the other.
I stood over on the left -
I didn't help my brother.

One day, my friend was hungry,
I gave him nothing to eat.
My friend said he was thirsty,
I didn't offer a drink.

I noticed all the strangers
But I didn't take them in,
I didn't want the bother,
It was too hard to begin.

Ignored the naked children
With their feet that had no shoes.
I walked right by the prison.
I had other things to do.

How can I love God, unseen,
When I don't love my brother?
Talk of love is just a lie
If we don't love each other.

Lord, please open up my eyes
To see the least of these.
Let me stand on Your right Hand
With those in whom You're pleased.

Matthew 25: 31 - 46

Walking, and leaping, and praising God

Walking, and leaping, and praising God -
I was lame from my mother's womb.
Hoping for coins or a crust of bread,
I was carried from room to room.

Walking, and leaping, and praising God -
I saw Peter and John walk by.
"Silver and gold have I none," they said,
"In the name of Jesus, arise!"

Walking, and leaping, and praising God -
They lifted me up by the hand.
For the first time my lame legs had strength.
For the first time, now I could stand.

Walking, and leaping, and praising God -
So into the temple I ran!
Everyone knew I was the cripple!
Amazed by what had just happened.

Abraham, Isaac, and Jacob's God
Descended to earthly sod.
He made a crippled man whole again -
Walking, and leaping, and praising God.

James 4:7

Satan appears as an angel of light,
Tempting with beautiful things.
All that he offers seems perfect and right,
And leads to death's horrible sting.

Satan offers the enticing, smooth road,
The way to your heart's desire.
Everything beautiful, pleasant and good,
Its ending is tormenting fire.

Satan's a liar from the beginning,
But all that he says seems true.
Deceiving, tricking us, leading away
From God's precious Word that is true.

He never uses the frightening things,
Ugly, revolting or bad.
His bait is always the things we want most
To catch us in his evil grasp.

God gave His weapon, the sword of His Word,
If we will just hold it high,
All Satan's lies will fall down in its light.
God's truth will reveal every lie.

Use every weapon that God has given.
Fight to hold onto His truth.
Use every weapon to break Satan's lies.
Resist him and he'll flee from you.

Deliverer

To fight an enemy stronger than you,
You need God's power to see you through.
The armor of God, covering you,
Then wait for Deliverer.

It doesn't matter if there's more of them.
It doesn't matter how many men.
God has ordained His victory when
You wait for Deliverer.

Ten thousand demons fall on your right hand,
Enemies rage but they'll never stand,
You have something that they'll never have.
You have the Deliverer.

You'll utterly conquer all of your foe.
You will succeed and will never be thrown.
You will go places they'll never go.
You'll go with Deliverer.

His Holy Hand is almighty to save,
His Holy Spirit makes fearful ones brave,
His awesome power conquered the grave -
Amazing Deliverer.

Delivered from evil on every side,
Delivered and pardoned - nothing to hide,
Delivered from death, now you arise
With Jesus, Deliverer.

Who You Are

Who You are, and where You are,
My God! So high above me.
Who I am and where I am –
Could You ever love me?

Yahweh, great I AM, alone,
Your white throne is in a place,
Carnal man could never reach –
Where no one sees Your Face.

God Almighty, Lord of all,
Your creation bows to you.
Holy wonder, majesty –
All praises sing to You.

What is man, that You should want
A dwelling place in his heart?
What's this dust that is below,
The holy God You are?

Created in Your image, all
The earth waits for redemption.
Crowned with glory, we will be
Sons of God You mention.

Holy One, Creator God
The power of life unfailing.
Given freely to the ones
Who call upon Your Name.

Mystery

What are Your secrets, Lord most high?
What are Your mysteries?
Why do you hide Yourself, O God,
Where human eyes can't see?

Within the flood, within the wind,
Within the hurricane.
A cloud by day, the fire by night,
The tempest and the rain.

In temples made of wood and stone,
In tents of cattle's skin,
An ark of wood encased with gold
Are places You have been.

You live no longer in a place
That's built by human hands.
This world we see does not contain
Jehovah, Great I AM.

Your Spirit whispers as the wind,
Through treetops to and fro.
The eyes of Jesus look out through
The least of these, I know.

I know Your secret, Lord most high,
I know Your mystery.
You hide Yourself inside my heart,
Where human eyes can't see.

Abraham

God spoke to Abraham words that were plain:
"Go up to the mountaintop.
Take your son, your only son,
And lay him upon a rock.

"Then offer your son, your dearly loved son,
As a sacrifice to Me."
God gives and He takes away,
As Abraham soon would see.

He raised his knife high above his son's head,
His tears rolled down to the ground.
"I've always obeyed you, Lord."
His sobs were the only sound.

Isaac was spared by a Voice from above:
Saying, "Do not harm your son.
Now I see inside your heart –
Obedience, unquestioned."

God sent a sacrifice, perfect and pure,
For fathers and sons, alike.
With absolute trust in Him,
All doubts we can lay aside.

If we do whatever God asks us to,
The outcome is in His Hands.
We have nothing left to fear,
His strength meets every demand.

Always there

When I through many storms have passed,
Am battered to and fro,
When sorrows fill my heart and soul,
I know not where to go,

My heart has overflowed with cares,
And troubles mount on me,
My tears have poured down like the rain,
Despair has victory.

My High Priest feels just what I feel,
The grief and the despair.
And even when I cannot see,
My God is always there.

His mighty Arms have held me up,
His great Hand has supplied.
His great power overcomes
The grip of Satan's lies.

The pain of living on this earth
Seems more than I can bear.
But I must keep my eyes on Him,
For He is always there.

No misery can hold me down,
No sin or earthly care.
No weapon of the enemy –
My God is always there.

Enough

God poured out His blessing on me,
His Holy Spirit, grace and love.
His Word He gives to me each day –
But it is not nearly enough.

I want more of You, my Master,
More blessing, more peace, and more love.
I cannot do without You, Lord –
Of You, I cannot get enough.

Give me everything You have, Lord,
Every blessing You have above,
Each fruit of Your Holy Spirit –
Because I still don't have enough.

As long as flesh is in control –
My human edges are still rough,
As long as sin is still in me,
I know I just don't have enough.

Until I'm face to Face with You,
Until I've finally learned to love,
When You've changed me in an instant –
Your presence, God, will be enough.

His Hands

Who can ever comprehend
The sovereign mind of God?
Who can claim to understand
The things that He has done?

Mortal minds – we cannot see
His power and mighty deeds.
Human hearts – they can't contain
His holy majesty.

He gives and He takes away
According to His plan.
He Who made the universe
Holds all things in His Hands.

Death and life are in His grip,
The light and darkness, too.
Joy and sorrow come from Him –
With all things, old and new.

Once you get your eyes on Him,
And finally you see,
Mighty God is over all,
And He has victory,

Human plans just fade away –
Our worries, cares, and strife.
Problems, troubles, tears and sins –
The burdens of this life.

God is over all of it,
God knows it all before.
God's Own Word has made it done –
He knows your heart, and more.

Human minds can't comprehend,
Our hearts can't understand.
I will rest in Him and know –
It's all within His Hands.

Luke 7:36-50

I clutched the alabaster box,
And stumbled down the street,
Blinded by tears I hurried on,
The Master I wanted to see.

Creeping in the Pharisee's house,
Not wanting to be seen,
Simon, a righteous man, I know
Would certainly ask me to leave.

When I was just a little girl,
To me, my grandma gave
The beautiful box of ointment,
For my wedding night to be saved.

All of my life I'd treasured it,
Even through all of my sin.
Even though no man wants me now,
I just want to give it to Him.

Ready with those at the table,
Jesus, there in His seat.
Seeing His precious Face moved me,
I trembled and started to weep.

Kneeling before Him I broke it,
My priceless, precious box.
I poured it on His Head and Feet,
And never once thought of the cost.

My hair tumbled down with my tears,
I wept and kissed His Feet.
In a room crowded with people,
It's only my Jesus and me.

Those painful regrets and sorrows,
Sin of a thousand years,
Mary, notorious harlot –
Washed away in perfume and tears.

Jesus, the words You spoke to me!
"Your sins are forgiven."
Simple words raised me to my feet,
And I caught a glimpse of heaven.

"Your faith has saved you; go in peace."
And His peace filled my soul.
Unshackled from my sin at last,
His loving mercy made me whole.

Who but He befriends the sinner?
Who wipes out guilt and shame?
Who is this Man who forgives sins?
Jesus Christ is His Name.

Liberty

When the iron door slams shut,
And the jailer locks me in,
And he claps the heavy chains
Tight around my legs and wrists,

I'm suddenly a prisoner,
I'm horrified at this fate,
Not knowing how I got here –
No one to open the gate.

Sin takes you so much farther
Than you ever want to go.
It costs you all that you have,
Then just leaves you all alone.

It's dark and damp and cold here,
There's no one to be my friend.
I can hear Satan laughing,
And my life seems at an end.

We're trapped in our own prisons,
And we ourselves have made them.
Locked inside our foolish sin,
And bound by chains of Satan.

There is One Who holds the key,
He's the One Who opens doors,
He shines light into the cell –
Releases captive prisoners.

Those walls aren't too strong for Him,
Chains He can easily break.
Gates open and you walk out.
You're the free one He has made.

Who He frees, is free indeed –
Never go back to that cell.
Take His Hand and walk away –
Jesus has freed you from hell.

His Heart

Walking with Jesus one day,
My sweet Savior took my hand,
"The Father now wants you to see
The things you don't understand."

I just sighed and shook my head,
How can the human mind hold
The knowledge and wonder of God?
They're beyond what we can know.

But Jesus showed me His Heart,
I wept when I looked inside.
It's filled with love for the world,
Top to bottom, side to side.

Love and mercy, grace and peace –
Patience like none on this earth.
Infinite blessings and pardon,
And all that I don't deserve.

Jesus, how can You love me?
I've nothing to offer You.
A wandering and sinful heart,
There's not much that I can do.

"My child, you are a treasure
Of such priceless worth to Me.
I'm willing to pay any cost
To have you in heaven with Me."

And pay the cost He has done.
He traded His life for mine.
All of my sins have been pardoned,
By love without measure or time.

I took the Hand of my Savior,
With joy and with gratitude.
Because He has shown me His Heart,
And everything in it is good.

Conformed to His image

When every piece has been blackened by the fire
that rains from God,
Removing the protection He once gave,
He beats us with His rod.

And our bloody bits are scattered from the pain
more than one night.
Bleeding out our sins and foolish natures,
We slowly become right.

Whom He loves, He chastens – He has told us this
so many times.
So, then we thank Him for these broken bones,
And He renews our minds.

When every human part is burned beyond ash,
flesh ripped away,
When every drop has been drained out of us,
Our shattered frames like clay –

There's finally room for God to work inside us,
for we are dead.
The carnal man of sin has been replaced
With Jesus Christ instead.

Pearl

Precious pearl of great price,
How I have searched for You.
Selling all that I have,
To purchase Your kingdom truth.

Leaving father and mother,
Brothers and sisters, too.
Leaving all that I own –
Exchanging it all for You.

I don't want earthly jewels,
I don't want costly gold.
I want the Pearl of truth,
To transform my human soul.

Lord God, I need Your wisdom,
Working inside my soul.
Showing me Your secrets,
Making my wounded heart whole.

God's kingdom is so priceless,
Worth everything I own.
I give my all to You,
For Your kingdom Pearl, alone.

The stone

Roll away the stone, Lord.
Its weight is far too much.
Human hands can't budge it.
My strength is not enough.

I am trapped behind it,
Still silent in this tomb.
Waiting for Your brilliance,
To penetrate this gloom.

Jesus, can You hear me?
I'm crying out to You.
Roll away the stone, Lord.
Please strengthen me anew.

I could grasp Your Hand, Lord,
If You could hear my shout,
The stone would roll away,
And You would pull me out.

You don't want Your people
In the dark, far from You.
You tore apart the veil,
So we could walk on through.

Roll away the stone, Lord.
Oh, roll it far away.
Resurrection life, Lord,
Is what I need today.

My prayer

Jesus, take my offering,
I pour it out for You.
I want to give You everything
These human hands can do.

Jesus, take this human life,
Exchange it for Your Own.
Please take my tears and suffering,
And make this heart Your home.

Jesus, I don't know why You
Would choose to live in me.
Or why a King would leave His throne,
To live in poverty.

With Your life, You've purchased me,
Your Word declares it's so.
The value that You see in me
Is something I can't know.

I will follow in Your steps,
I'll go where You have led.
I want the new life that You give –
The old man to be dead.

Use me any way You can,
I give my all to You.
I want to hear the words, "Well done,"
When this, my life, is through.

Presence

Do you feel His presence -
Almighty God, in you?
Do you hear Him whisper -
Holy words of truth?

Can you see His beauty,
Revealed in every day?
Feel His Holy Spirit,
Helping on the way?

Do you feel Him near you?
Closer than a brother,
Dearer than a friend, and
Sweeter than a lover?

Can you find Him in you?
In every secret place,
Wanting to befriend you,
And see you Face to face.

God came down from heaven,
And came to you and me.
He is always with us,
He will never leave.

God is here beside you,
He's that still, small Voice.
Filling you with power,
Giving you His joy.

God's Arms are around you,
They hold you tenderly.
He is ever with you,
He will never leave.

Psalm 2012

With my voice I cried out to God,
But He did not answer me.
With my words I begged Him to come,
But He didn't hear me, or speak.

I groaned deep within my soul,
I filled my room with screams.
I am completely unable
To breach this wall between.

Holy, sovereign God, and
Sinful, foolish man.
How can we ever hear Him?
How can we understand?

His thoughts are far above our thoughts,
Our human ears cannot hear God.
Lord, I long to know You,
I am desperate for Your touch.

My soul cries out for You, my God.
I am desperate for Your Voice.

Please don't leave Your servant here alone,
I need You more than anything.
I cannot live without You.
Without You, I can't breathe.

Hear my cry, O Lord.
From the depths of my soul,
From the belly of hell,
Do I cry unto You.

My God

As long as I live, I'll sing praise to my God,
The maker of heaven and earth.
My heart will sing every praise known to Him.
My mouth tells His glorious worth.

If I remain silent, the rocks will cry out.
All creation praises on high.
The glorious universe, sun and stars,
Throughout all His kingdom they cry.

Who made heaven and earth and all they contain.
Created man in His image,
Who speaks to the humble, lowliest ones.
Glory to God in the highest!

Who sends forth angels as His messengers,
Imparting His words to mankind.
Who crowns man with glory, honor and light,
Throughout all creation He shines.

Majesty, honor, might, glory and power,
To God in the highest, above.
Wisdom and honor, strength, blessing and praise.
Holiness, reverence, and love.

Holy

The hundred and forty-four thousand,
Clothed in the Lord's righteousness.
Stand and cry, "Holy, Lord!"
These are the ones He purchased.

Their white robes are spotless and shining,
The righteousness of the saints,
Angels cry "Holy, Lord!"
For these all creation waits.

Worshiping the Lamb upon the throne,
Brilliant, the sun on my face.
There is none beside You,
Yesterday, today, always.

He alone is holy, only He.
More holy than we can know.
Clothed in spotless beauty,
Creation falls at His throne.

Standing all around the sea of glass,
And all our crowns we've cast down.
All tribes, tongues and nations,
"Holy, Lord! Holy!" the sound.

Salvation to God upon the throne,
Power, glory, praise, strength, might!
Holy, holy, holy!
Shining city's only light.

The Face of Jesus

Just a glance, while sitting at His Feet,
Just a glimpse of glory, incomplete,
Just a momentary flash of light –
I see the Face of Jesus.

Angels leaping, dancing near His throne,
His Eyes and thoughts remain with me alone,
And all my secret places, He has known.
All in the Face of Jesus.

At His Feet I cast my every care,
And all my thoughts and burdens with Him share.
Contentment, joy and peace I have found there –
There at the Feet of Jesus.

And why would I return back to the earth?
My soul within has finally found her worth,
And sin and darkness have no place to work
Here at the Feet of Jesus.

The Master smiles at me so tenderly,
His delight I am, I plainly see.
His grace and beauty all envelop me.
The precious Face of Jesus.

What the Lord has done

Heaven's brilliant light, overcoming darkness.
Golden grace poured out like warmth of summer sun.
Peace that passes understanding fills my soul.
A precious glimpse of what the Lord has done

Wisdom from above, beyond the human mind.
Understanding, doors unlocking one by one.
Mysteries revealed, and knowledge yet deeper.
The secrets shown of what my Lord has done.

Resurrection power bursts from silent graves.
The blood of Jesus defeated death, and won.
What's impossible with man is done with God,
And all will see the miracles He's done.

Death, where's your victory? Hell, where is your sting?
The race before us in victory we will run.
There's no turning back from what He's called us to,
No mind can grasp the things the Lord has done.

The heavy cross

Punishment greater than I can bear.
Its weight presses me to the ground.
I stumble beneath these endless cares,
And pray that some help may be found.

As He is, so are we in the earth.
His cross was carried on broken Skin.
His tears fell like rain upon the dirt.
A heavy load of human sin.

Why, oh, why is there no other way?
Why must I bleed and hang so long?
Crying to heaven day after day.
Suffering and sorrow, no more song.

Jesus, Savior, I go where You go,
I'm giving myself up for You.
The cross tears away all that I know,
Destroys everything that I do.

When all of my life has drained away,
When everything fleshly is gone,
Humanity's veil is ripped away,
The cross has made right every wrong.

Oh, my Jesus! Just to be like You!
My simple heart's cry every day.
The heavy cross reveals You to me,
There simply is no other way.

Silence

In silence the earth was created.
God moved over the waters.
Out of silence the heavens were birthed -
Universe, sun, moon and stars.

In silence He tells me His secrets,
When madness smothers my mind.
Out of darkness His light pierces through,
Reveals what I couldn't find.

In silence we're waiting for Jesus.
Stilling each thought of the flesh.
Surrendering all to His purpose,
Washed in His spirit afresh.

In silence my Master comes to me,
When I can't utter a word.
When all of my human plans crumble,
His Voice I have finally heard.

The lost sheep

I wandered away, just wandered away,
I spied the greener grass.
I wandered away, just wandered away.
I never thought to ask.

At first I was fine, everything sweet,
Gazing at all I see.
Suddenly cold, and suddenly dark,
Suddenly no one with me.

Lost and alone, frightened and cold,
Wounded and lonely was I.
So far from home, so all alone,
The path I couldn't find.

Faintly, so faintly, I heard His sweet Voice,
Shepherd, Savior, and Friend.
I stumbled toward Him, exhausted and hurt.
Into His Arms I went.

He held me gently, tenderly carried
His wandering sheep back home.
He bandaged my wounds, spoke softly to me,
No more afraid and alone.

Jesus, I love You, Savior, I need You.
I'll no more wander away.
You rescued me, healed me, carried me home.
Forever with You I will stay.

The good Samaritan

Enemies sworn, for life.
Jews and Samaritans.
Looking the other way,
Turning our backs on them.

The world doesn't need them –
Different, shabby, unclean.
Keep them in the shadows.
Unheard, unknown, unseen.

Walking to Jericho,
In the blink of an eye,
Beaten and stripped of all,
Thrown to the dust, to die.

Dimly, through darkness, pain,
Aware of passersby,
No strength to lift my head,
Too wounded now, to cry.

One of those people stopped,
Gently bandaged my wounds,
Lifted me in his arms,
Carried me to a room.

Memories – sorrow and shame.
All my past bigotry.
Priest and Levite passed on,
My own didn't help me.

Rescued by stranger – foe.
Shown kindness, undeserved.
Mercy flowed over me,
And brotherhood was birthed.

God's servants – everywhere.
Places we least expect.
Let's go and do likewise.
Because we have been blessed.

Suicide Bible

You came back to church.
You'd been gone for a long time.
I remembered you – your handsome, smiling face.
I was glad you came.

When it was over, you met me in the parking lot.
You said you remembered me, too.
You handed me that brand-new Bible,
And we stood in the October leaves.

Why did you do it, Joel*?
I'm old enough to be your mom,
I'm someone you barely know.
I was humbled and touched by your gift.

You said the Lord told you to give it to me.
Maybe you saw the battered one I carry,
And felt sorry for me.
We hugged as darkness fell, and went our ways.

Two days later we all got the news.
She stood up front and told us as her tears rained down.
You were found in a pool of blood
On the bathroom floor.

Why did you do it, Joel?
Why did you listen to the voice of the destroyer?
Why did you smile in church, and give me a Bible?
I don't understand.

You could have had everything.
He had a plan for you.
He loved you then, and didn't stop -
Despite what you did.

I never read that Bible.
I don't want to touch it.
I'm sad when I look at it.
Why did you do it, Joel?

*Not his real name

Step of faith

How can I move forward?
The path is blocked and broken.
How do I keep going?
And do the things You've spoken?

Every door seems shut now.
The light I had has gone dark.
Everyone seems gone now.
No one to show me the mark.

I'm trudging on this path
Day after day after day,
Never really knowing
If I have lost my way.

So many years ago,
The word of God came to me,
Giving me instructions,
Of what my walk should be.

Jehovah never changes,
I AM will never turn.
His word is always constant.
My wandering heart must learn.

Though it is dark and lonely,
Though I can't see the way,
Although my feet still stumble,
Yet on His road I'll stay.

Jehovah never changes.
He told me what to do.
By faith I will obey Him,
And He will see me through.

the lion/THE LION

You just roam around
Roaring, threatening, scaring us,
Seeking your advantage,
Seeking whom you may devour.
You try to find an opening,
Accuse us night and day –
And then you spring.

But Jesus is THE LION
Of the tribe of Judah.
He will drive you out,
And you will run away.
You're nothing but a coward,
And He's defeated you
By His own Word.

I need never fear you –
Pathetic, miserable worm.
My shield has blocked your darts
And I've sliced you with my sword.
My LION nullified you –
Stopped your dirty game
And all you do.

A stone

Am I a stone?
Do these calamities roll off me
Like drops of rain?
Do these curses not absorb
Nor cause me pain?

Am I a rock?
When icy winds swirl down upon me
Do I not feel?
Disaster's heavy weight won't
Force me to kneel?

Am I so hard
That Satan's arrows cannot pierce me?
I feel no need?
Disemboweled by Satan's thrusts
And never bleed?

I'm not a stone.
Not unflinching in the face of hurt.
Not strong or brave.
Yet doing battle ceaselessly –
My crown to save.

I'm not a rock.
I'm not untouched by slings and arrows.
With broken bones
And battle scars I stand here.
I'm still Your Own.

Just Your servant,
Occupying until You return.
Though I'm weeping,
I know You have my life
In Your safe keeping.

Looking upward,
Desperate for a glimpse of heaven's plan.
Waiting for You.
I know that my Redeemer lives,
And He is true.

Job 6:12

Tender love

Expressions of the human heart –
Inadequate and frail.
Laying carnal thoughts aside,
I peer behind the veil.

Lover of my soul, my King,
Redeemer, ever true.
Purchased by His life, I am
Reborn and made anew.

How can human tongues express
A love beyond the mind?
A love so great He died the death
That certainly was mine.

Tender love, redeeming love,
Unfailing love is He.
Jesus, Savior, precious One,
His love has rescued me.

He pulls me ever closer
And I rest in His embrace.
No turning back for me, not now,
I see Him Face to face.

Him

When you see it,
When you finally understand
The price He paid,
All the treasures of this life,
All the things that mattered
Just fade away.

When you know Him,
When you join with Him in death
To all you are,
All the obstacles are gone,
All excuses vanish
Within your heart.

Walking with Him,
Understanding why He bled
And tore the veil.
Holding to His promises,
Remembering His word –
You will prevail.

Living for Him,
Disregarding human plans
You walk alone.
Daily picking up that cross,
You're walking where He walked
And heading home.

When you see Him,
In the twinkling of an eye
You will be changed.
Human, overlaid with gold.
The mystery finished,
To die is gain.

Beautiful obedience

You are beautiful beyond description,
I reach out for You.
There is only one way,
I must obey.

Your value cannot be calculated,
I give all for You.
To see you Face to face,
I must obey.

Beautiful obedience – so priceless!
It takes me closer.
The road gets narrower
As I obey.

Light reveals more light with each step I take,
Becoming like You.
My self diminishing,
When I obey.

Obedience learned by what You suffered,
I walk the same path.
You are my Example.
My Lord obeyed.

The carpenter

He made things out of wood,
He started young.
In Galilee He worked –
God's only Son.

He carved and cut and sawed
At Joseph's side.
A son of carpenters –
Another kind.

He befriended sinners.
They followed Him.
With love He captured them –
Forgave their sin.

One word from Him would change
A human soul.
Transformed with power divine –
He made them whole.

He makes things out of wood,
He does it still.
He chisels flesh away –
Perfects our will.

He makes things out of wood –
Makes new from old.
From fallen man to Him –
From wood to gold.

Risen

It is so dark and cold here,
And I am afraid.
I stumble along the path,
Not sure of the way.

The world is gray and silent
In this awful spring.
I waited for this hour.
The spices to bring.

But the stone is rolled away,
He's no longer there.
One more sorrow heaped on me
I cannot bear.

Where have they taken my Lord?
Through tears I ask why.
My Savior, my Precious Love –
I watched Him die.

Wasn't His murder enough?
The nails and insults?
Whoever stole Him away
Has torn my heart.

Mary.

Can it be?
My Master! My Teacher!
It is He!

Messiah! I should have known!
He raised my brother.
The Resurrection and Life,
There is no other.

The tomb of death is empty.
I will no longer
Seek the living among the dead.
For He is not here,
He is risen, as He said.

The "bastard"

A quiet life, alone,
Misunderstood.
A little child, they said
He was no good.

His friends were few, they were
Outcasts, like Him.
Sons of drunks and harlots,
With futures dim.

No one wants to be near
A bastard child.
No hand of friendship out
To one defiled.

And yet, He grew, and learned
The things of God.
A so-called bastard sprung
From Jesse's rod.

His friends are few, they are
The least of these.
Unwanted and unloved,
His mercy sees.

His Father was above,
Though no one knew.
Born of a virgin's womb –
For me and you.

The beauty of your absence

When you come to me with all your tricks,
Your persuasive power and your lies.
I wrap myself in His truth and claim
The greater power of Jesus Christ.

When you sneak and start your whispering,
And lean a little closer still,
I grasp my sword and hold it higher –
And thrust you through by Jesus' will.

When I least suspect it, there you are.
Your lying mouth and ugly face.
My shield is up and my shoes are on,
For I intend to win this race.

I nearly laugh each time you show up.
You still can't see He's my defense.
I rest in Him, and you disappear.
Peace - the beauty of your absence.

Bread

Bread of heaven,
Living Bread,
Truly satisfies.
All who hunger for this Bread
Will have their needs supplied.

With daily Bread,
Feed me, Lord
Fresh and new, I pray.
Fill me, Lord - I'm empty now.
Fill me every day.

You never fail,
Living Bread,
Daily Bread, for me.
Broken Bread is my desire,
Lord, fill all of me.

Questions/Answers

How far can I go with You, Jesus?
How long does Your path extend?
How many miles will You take me?
When will I see the end?

What lies ahead in the distance?
When does Your Light break through?
When is the darkness defeated?
When will my journey be through?

Is there an end to this trouble?
A place where sorrows will cease?
A road that leads to the quiet?
A path that leads me to peace?

I'll go to the end with You, Jesus.
I'll walk till I see Your Light.
I'll use all the strength that You've given,
I will fight the good fight.

Mile after mile we will travel,
You'll not let go of my hand.
Together we'll go all the distance.
By grace, able to stand.

The joy of the Lord is my strength.
He has selected the Way,
And He is directing my steps,
My task is just: Obey.

In heaven

In heaven there's no preaching,
No exhorting,
No rebuke.
In heaven no one's searching
For the truth.

In heaven there's no building,
There's no planning,
No resolve.
In heaven there's no riddle
To be solved.

In heaven there is worship,
Only worship,
Night and day.
All saints and angels shouting
Out His Name.

Only praises to the King,
Only music,
Only song.
And joyous adoration
All day long.

In heaven there's just praising,
Glorifying
Jesus Christ.
All creation bows to Him
Who is our Life.

In heaven there is worship,
Only worship,
Endless days.
And every voice rings out in
Ceaseless praise.

For Who You are

All that I have, I give,
Each breath, each moment lived.
My shallow human gifts,
For Who You Are.

You loved me first, so I
Will love You till I die.
My soul within me cries
For Who You Are.

All praise and majesty,
All worship to the King,
All of creation sings
To Who You Are.

'Thank You' is not enough
For Your unfailing love,
Your ways – so far above –
That's Who You Are.

I praise Your holy Name,
All saints will do the same,
Jehovah, yet unchanged,
I AM, You Are.

Dressed in glory

Washed, and cleansed, and purified,
Dressed in glory, at His side,
A spotless, holy, perfect bride –
That's how the Savior sees me.

Purged from all humanity,
Clothed with His humility,
A brilliant light for all to see –
It's Jesus shining through me.

Rising from the grave with Him,
Nailing to the cross, my sin,
Releasing self and human whims –
That's what my Lord did for me.

Kings and priests, we're seated now
At His right Hand, and nations bow,
With every tongue proclaiming how
He made His people holy.

Dressed in glory, evermore,
We cast our crowns and kneel before
The risen, holy, righteous Lord –
Emmanuel, our King.

Dead men's bones

So lovely on the outside –
So refined.
So polished and so perfect,
Brilliant shine.

The inward parts are stinking,
Rotten flesh.
Corruption and decay
And constant death.

Your life is like a graveyard
Someone tends.
With grass and trees and flowers,
Sun and wind.

Your soul is filled with evil –
Things long dead.
With brittle bones all scattered
End to end.

Who do you think you're fooling?
Jesus knows.
Black wretchedness inside where
No one goes.

So lovely on the outside –
All admire.
So putrid on the inside –
Satan's fire.

I know
(for Manuela, my sister in Christ)

I was your mother long ago,
I didn't know.
The gift of God so freely given -
I let go.
I never held your hand,
I didn't know.
I didn't understand,
So I let go.
My precious child, forgive me
In my pain.
Let healing come to us
Like heaven's rain.
I was your mother long ago,
And I still am.
Safe in the Arms of Jesus,
You hold His Hand.
And I will see you soon
And you will know,
How much I love you still
For now, I know.

Don't worry

It doesn't matter what you did
Or where you went.
It doesn't matter why or how -
The time you spent.
No one accuses you -
Of anything.
No one holds you hostage
To the blame.
Just turn around,
That's all.
Just turn around.
Just go to Him and prove
The lost is found.
He waits for you, oh yes,
He longs for you.
Forgiveness freely dealt -
Forever true.
Don't worry what they'll say
Or how things look.
Don't imagine sorrows Jesus took.
Surrender human pride and human plans.
Remember He is God, and you're a man.
Return and start again, this time with Him.
His mercy has forgotten all your sin.

For Isaiah

I prayed for you, my sweet, my precious son.
I prayed that God would give you to me.
Every day I thanked Him that you came.
Isaiah was your name.

I prayed that you would grow, be strong, be wise.
I prayed that we would talk together.
Every day I thanked Him for your life,
And wished you would arrive.

I prayed when your safe home began to crack,
I prayed and asked God to stay His Hand.
It was much too soon for you to be,
And yet you came to me.

I prayed when I looked down at your sweet face.
Fingers, toes, eyes and nose, arms and legs.
Perfectly flawless, and perfect form -
Died before you were born.

I prayed and asked God why He ripped away
My answered prayer, my heart, my own flesh.
Incredible joy, realized dreams,
Then my prayers turned to screams.

I prayed, beseeched my God to heal my mind –
Remove the madness caused by this breach.
Betrayal of all requests I'd made –
Yet madness still remained.

Could I go back, and make you never be?
And never have to feel this despair?
And never see your beautiful face?
While forfeiting His grace?

I prayed and wrestled with the Most High God,
With pain caused by blinded human eyes.
Giving anything to have you live,
Till nothing left to give.

In the end, I prayed again for strength,
Knowing I would never understand.
I buried you beneath a big tree –
And buried part of me.

I prayed that He would bring you back someday,
You'd be in the cloud of witnesses.
You'd come back with Him, and I'd see you,
And marvel how you grew.

God answers every prayer His people send.
He gives and takes away, every day.
Even through our madness we can see
His holy mystery.

For Zach

A tree of love grew by the river,
Grew straight and strong.
A polished arrow for our quiver,
Carried along.

God remembered all your mother's prayers,
Father's prayers too.
We were weighted down with many cares,
So He sent you.

Children are a blessing from the Lord,
How you blessed us!
Everything we wanted, and much more,
Hope sprung from dust.

God's Hand has been on you from the start,
Because we prayed.
You were born inside our waiting hearts,
And there you stayed.

Carefully, we'll aim, and then release,
Our shining star.
Sailing high and swift above the trees –
You will go far.

Psalm 127: 3 – 5

For Jenna

You exist above, in my mind's eye,
In that secret place that no one knows.
My beauty, grace and joy divine –
Precious daughter of mine.

You dance, a twirling ballerina,
In pink lace and fancy satin shoes.
I scoop you up and kiss your neck,
And breathe your every breath.

You came and went so very quickly,
Before I had a chance to meet you,
You grew for such a little while –
Your presence made me smile.

My tears poured down again for children
Chosen by God to simply pass through.
Never having blooms or flowers,
Life in days and hours.

Another silent dream laid to rest,
Another gift returned to Sender,
You walked through the door He gave –
Something beyond the grave.

On a sunny day beside the sea
You died despite my finest efforts.
You became a part of the sand.
You hold Isaiah's hand.

Mothers

Mothers, hold your babies –
Hold them near.
Comfort them and chase away their fears.
Sing to them through every restless night.
Drive away the darkness –
Bring them light.

Mother, hold your small one –
Take his hand.
He is not too young to understand.
The love of Jesus he receives from you,
Enables him to grow –
With faith anew.

Mothers, hold your children –
Make them strong.
The battle for their souls is fierce and long.
Train them in the way that they should go,
So they will not depart –
This we know.

Mothers, hold them now –
And please don't wait.
Tomorrow comes, and then it is too late.
In a whisper, in a moment, they are gone.
They're all grown up, and
They are far from home.

The baby that you held
With so much pride?
He's now a man –
His wife is at his side.
Oh, mothers, hold them now –
And evermore.

Children are a blessing from the Lord.

First in line

When they start coming for us –
God's people rounded up.
When guillotines are sharpened,
When there is no more time –
Let me be first in line.

When the saints are slaughtered
For conforming to His name,
Beheaded for His glory,
And charged with trumped-up crimes,
Let me be first in line.

There is no greater honor
Than to walk the road He walked.
His fellowship of suffering,
The human, made Divine.
Let me be first in line.

The witness of my Jesus,
The wrath His name incurs,
Fury of Satan's forces
Unleashed on those who shine –
Let me be first in line.

When martyrs' blood starts flowing,
Executed for His cause,
May my life be read by all.
My life, no longer mine.
Let me be first in line.

Revelation 20:4

My crown

I never wanted it;
I walked away.
My selfish thoughts came in –
"Too much to pay."
I didn't ask for it,
It was too hard.
I couldn't pay the cost
Of tears and blood.
But still it beckoned me,
That glittering crown.
I saw it far away
And turned around.
Couldn't do without it
Despite the cost.
To claim it as my own,
To find the lost.
It cost me everything –
All that I had.
It emptied me of all
Yet made me glad.
When He gave it to me,
"Well done," I heard.
My life's work simply summed
With His two words.

Stand

When all is said and done, who will stand?
And who will win and touch the Master's Hand?
Will those who have great schemes and plots succeed?
Or those who cried to Him on bended knees?

When all is said and done, who will see?
Who will know the truth and be made free?
Who will see the Savior face to Face?
And who will benefit from matchless grace?

When I have done all that I can, I'll stand.
When I've said the final word, I'll take His Hand.
When persecution mounts on every side,
I will not stop my run against the tide.

The race is not to swift or strong of heart.
The prize is not awarded to the smart.
But those who persevere until the end –
Will find a lasting crown upon their heads.

Having done all, with nothing left,
I'll continue standing
Till my last breath.